Expressions of Life

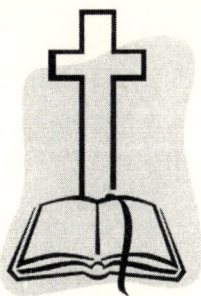

Expressions of Life

Poetry With A Message
Of
Life, Love and Care

Frances Wright

To order additional copies of this book, contact:
Xlibris Corporation
1-888-795-4274
www.Xlibris.com
Orders@Xlibris.com
109723

Contents

Dedication

This book is dedicated to the siblings of Leroy
and Verdell MC Millian.
Rutha Mae, Johnny Lee, Elnora, Jack, Mark, Annie Doris,
Loretta, and Mazola. All Grand Children and (Great
Great . . .) Aunt Classie, Aunt Dora and Uncle Frank. The
Holy Tabernacle Church Family.

Preface

Expressions of life is exactly what the title indicates,
and every poem is meant to do just that. Everyday we
encounter people in our journey of life that either inspire
us or amaze us in some way. Wisdom is imparted or
foolishness amuse us, we are encouraged or torn down.
Let these short messages be the fluoroscope of the soul
not to condemn anyone but to see Gods view point.
Therefore Poetry With A Message will have
achieved its objective.

Acknowledgments

Life expressions is a culmination of the wisdom God has allowed me to observe while dealing with people he has placed in my life and around it. The messages are meant to display the knowledge of Gods word. I give thanks to him and the many teachers he's used to get his word to me. I would also like to give thanks to the many people who recognized Gods creativity in me and their encouragement that produced this book, mainly my church family at Holy Tabernacle and my four children. Special thanks to both my former and present Pastors who allowed me to share my Poetry in special services.
Thank You

Foreword

Everyone's life story is someone else's life story also. The names maybe different but the characteristics bear so many similarities. Their location of the experiences may denote a dimension of many miles a part or a different season of change, birthday or year and still connect them to the experience. Fame or fortune maybe an issue but maybe of no importance when the story is shared. Life is lived from birth to death. What really matters is who is living it through you, Christ or Satan? Yes it matters whom it is rooted in. From my childhood experiences even until this present time I was aware there was a greater power than what I experienced or saw with my natural eyes. The struggles of myself image and what others thought placed a demand upon my personal look that was often unbearable. Later In life as I came to know Christ as my all and all I began to cast my cares upon him. Through an anointed man of God I learned that God has endowed all men with at least one talent or gift. So out of inspiration and my love of poetry this desire to relate to others, Poetry With A Message was born.

The Living Christ

Oh how I sought to know Him
I wanted to see him as he is,
Not just through mortal eyes.
I searched for him by reading
Many, many tries, hour and upon hours.
I obtained volumes of knowledge.

But now I realize that the search
To find had all been his.
Surprising he had given me my desire.
It was his longing in my heart
His faith was given to me to believe
Every thought of action in took,
He had let me conceive.

To see him, I had to look beyond
The creature and see the Creator
Of all things great and small
I looked beyond the world of matter
To the realm of spirit to the One
Who is all and in all.

The Word of the Bible had to come alive,
To reveal the one within
Now I know without a doubt
He is the one who was, who is
And will always be. Search him out.

Christ is life love and peace. He is alive, willing and able to be all and all for us. He has always been here for us. It was him seeking us all the time. He loves us with an everlasting love. I am so glad to know his as the one who is and was forevermore

John 1:1-9, Rev1:8,11

If Only

Only two words, how well they are used,
Overworked are they, yet poorly the most excused
If only some say I could sing, I'll sing to
Build up the church service, Nobody will have to ask me to.
If only I could speak well, I'll witness for Jesus
By all means that's what I will do.
Some say if I only had some talent
I wouldn't let it go to waste
I'll work to develop it and use it for the Lord.
I'll put my time in now with all my might in haste.
Some say if I only had some money
To the Lord's service I would give,
There are so many needs, how for him I would like to contribute,
But since only a few dollars I do have,
I need it for to live.
Why don't we stop saying "if only"
And use what we have to use,
Yes it's been so overworked but still poorly excused.

Don't build your life on "if only". It's only an illusion and will get you nowhere. It's also like living in a dream world that never comes to pass

1 Peter 1:3,4,9,10

What's In It For Me?

Some folks never want to give anything for free,
There is always the question "What's in it for me?"
They always want you to contribute to their support,
But when you need them they are the very ones to cry broke.
They gripe and groan, such sigh of relief,
When you are finally gone you had asked them to help you out,
All you got was argument and pouts.
No matter how you beg and plead,
They just cannot see the need
Even if there is no money to pay the bills,
What do they care as long as they have their fill.
Work they never will, but oh how they make use of the things you build,
You must go on don't despair
For there will always be those with "What's in it for me?" their only care.

We should never be just concerned about ourselves. The Word of God exhorts us to esteem others more highly than ourselves and put others needs' before our own.

1 John 3:11, 1 John 4:7,8

You Can Make It

You may not always have a song in your heart,
Peace may be a treasure you haven't got
But listen you don't have to sink under the burden of sin
You can make it if you just let Jesus in.
Though life seems complicated to you,
Seek God and live for he is the life, the way and the truth
He has the answer to every problem
And the wisdom to see you through,
You can make it no matter how dark the day,
Just listen to his word and do as it say,
God and his work is one in the same
Yes you can make it. Glory to his holy name.

God has a plan for each life, only through him can it be accomplished. His ability equips you to fulfill the plan as well as bring the joy of a fulfilled life. Yes you will make it

Phil 4:13, 4:4

My First Impression

Sister M and Sister C, two sisters from the local church, got together for tea on afternoon, and oh it really brought the light out in their lives so very, very, much, their conversation went such and such . . .
Sister M to Sister C said you know I really admire you so very, very, much. My life you have so deeply touched. But Sister, let me tell you this haven't always been my opinion of you. The words I am about to say is really true. I had my first impression, mind you. You see I am a pretty good judge of character for I have the spirit of discerning rather girl. When I first heard you teach, I though within myself, she should really work on her speech. Oh there was so many other things I saw through the spirit, mind you. But in time I grew to love and appreciate you. Just how much, only God knows.

Sister C waited patiently for her chance to talk. I am glad I have helped you in your Christian walk. My first impression of you I didn't trust. For I am not one to accept everything that pops into my mind or anyone I hear talk. What I observe about you wasn't kind. I always ask God to guide my mind, I ask him to let me see people as he sees them and to always be loving and kind. When I tried to pray that prayer concerning you, I drew a blank. How peculiar too, now I know the reason and to God be thanks. I saw you look at me from head to feet, what you saw God and you only knew. I now know your defeat. But God's spirit didn't give you that discernment, your carnal flesh was at work. For God's spirit is never wrong and his thoughts are not as such you alone did interpret.

Message—Judge not that we be judge the scripture says. We do well to take hold of this admonition. If we take heed to our mouth we keep our souls from much trouble.

Matt7:1, Romans 14, 1 Cor 4:3,4

Evil Report

Negative words spoken against
The words of God are evil.
The Bible so plainly speaks
These evil words will control your life
Whether you be Jew, Gentile or Greek.

It seems the world enjoys the evil report
It's broadcasted in our daily news
But, I will choose the things of God any day
I am given the choice to choose

Death and live is in the power of tongue
It takes the Spirit of God to control its use
Without the spirit control its
A powerful dynamite
A ready ligthted fuse.

To stay in tune with God, we must think on the things of God. The world is geared toward negativity. Death and life is in the power of the tongue is a spiritual truth and it is manifesting in the experiences of life daily. Choose life and live a good life. It is God's perfect plan.

Psalm 34:134, Matthew 12:37, Matthew 5:37

The Word of Life

The word of life is my all and all
A gift I received,
Valuable above all other treasures I possess
Great or small.

How glad I am the Word of Life
One day sought my dead soul
He purged my being of the evil within
Quickening me and making me whole.

The word of life continually
Makes me strong,
By it I can conquer all battles, overcome all wrong.

Fear is no longer a threat
For I am never left alone.
He indwells me,
Causes me to be free
Yet I am glad to know
To him I belong.

God's word is spirit and it is life. Choose God's life by choosing his word that covers the type of life you want to experience. We partake of his divine nature through the great and precious promise. Deny yourself and take all of him through his word. Death is the avenue to life, his cross and resurrection will provide everything for his provision is complete.

Proverbs 6:2, 10:19, 5:7, 4:5, Psalm 19:14

It's The Long Tongue

It's the long tongue that destroys left and right
Driving the choices of friends from our sight
That pink little instrument will cause many to cry
Moan, groan or sigh, or end up with black eyes

It's the long tongue that kills, it will kill or make you well
And make you glad or make you sad,
It will speak good as well as bad,
Lift up or tear down,
Make others don't want to be around

It's the tongue that confesses the truth or expresses the lie
Speak love words or cause you to sin curse or judge
It can heal others or destroy their name, bless or make the shame
It can be like a gun or a stick of dynamite
Shooting and blowing up if not controlled through the Holy Spirit might.

It's the long tongue that will go in all direction
It needs sometime to be corrected it must be disciplined
So it will know when where and how to speak words at all times.
The wisdom of God will feed your mind
You will know when to be quiet because foolishness may cause the tongue
to get cut out

So use discretion as you speak, use it wisely don't be a fool
Remember God's golden rule, love others as thyself, be considerate above
all else.

Message—The wonder ability to speak is a God-given gift. We must not abuse it. It contains death and life. Many have been slain by its deadly poison. Many now live because of a spoken word.

James 3.

I Ain't The One

Sis J and Sis W from church together they walked,
Sis J pouted as they talked trying to cover up what was really in her heart,
tried to act naturally but it's easy to perform the hypocrite part.
Sis J said to Sis W, I ain't the one for sowing discord you know its true,
But you should have heard those remarks Sis R made about you.
I ain't the one for gossiping, it's not right for a saint to do
But girl let me tell you to her husband she sure ain't been true.
I ain't the one for being prejudice and of people making a distinction, for I am
not the one for causing a whole lot of contention. But you better watch her,
she ain't your friend, you stick with me I'll be with you clean to the end.
I ain't the one for giving advice especially if somebody didn't ask you, it
ain't nice, but let me tell you what I will do if it was me instead of you,
I'll let her know the things she is saying ain't so.
Butt out of my affairs before she finds herself missing some of that pretty
hair.
Now I ain't the one for violence I got my pride,
In my heart I have love and don't want to injure another's life
But this is one thing I just would take in stride,
Here she comes now, quick take my knife.
I ain't the one to hold a grudge
So what I am saying of me please don't misjudge,
But you are not the only one she made look bed,
She stole the only man I ever had!

Conversation is said to be the fluoroscope of the soul. We should listen carefully before engaged ourselves to it. God gave us two ears and one mouth. That means we should listen twice as much as we speak.

I Peter 4:9, James 5:9, Psalm 59:15

You Gotta Love

You got to love the devil out of
Some folks, they are as mean as can be
They enjoy being difficult you see
They can't stand good treatment, kindness just tears them up

They love to give out insults
But cant take a thing
You stand up to them
They become another man in a boxing ring

They are selfish and everything revolve around themselves,
There is no room for others in their world,
No, no one else

You gotta love them anyway
You got a task on your hand
Our god will help you to stand
Love them so until they becomes God's man

Message—love is the greatest defense against evil for it never faileth

1 Cor 13

There Is Work To Do

Why spend time in idleness?
There is so much to do
God has a special job just for you.
You were born for a purpose
Charted by God,
Directed toward his aim.
He gave you your heritage,
Your abilities to proclaim.
Get up and prepare yourself
There is a spot for you
That can be filled by no one else.
Let God lead you.
Depend wholly upon him in all your ways.
He will turn your idleness into busy days.

It has been said an idle mind is the devil's workshop. But the word of God says as a man thinketh in his heart, so is he. We can be successful as we mediate upon his word day and night. We will have his wisdom and find his purpose for us and his will. Only then can we be fulfilled.

Proverbs 19:15, Exodus 5:17, Matthew 20:3

Love Has a Language Of Its Own

Love has a language of its own
Lost in the ecstasy of his love,
When newly married she was so secure
She was his queen, his sweet thing his joy,
His baby and his sugar mama from heaven above
Like honey out of a dripping rocks freely flowed his words
He was her knight in shining armor,
Her tall dark and handsome
Who held the key to her everlasting heart,
The one who had chosen her to be his wife out of all the other women.
The one God had just for her as it should have been,
She didn't have to think twice.
But as time went by, they began to be less considerate of each other
And she became more and more like his mother.
The language began to change,
To woman, baldhead, fat, and even sometimes witch,
I shouldn't have married you, you make me sick.
She came up with some choice words of her own,
Big head, bossy, know-it-all,
I no longer want this home.
You used to be so loving and sweet
I loved you so much at times I couldn't eat
I am taking the kids, I am going to leave
I don't want anything you got, just allotment and child support will be fine
Don't try to get in touch with me, the child welfare agency will drop you
a few lines
All this came about because they stopped being kind
When the love language stop
You will lose what you got

*Message—It took love to get you a spouse. Love will continue to light the
flame, for love surpasses all things.*

1 Cor 7, Eph 5:23-30

The Blessing

Brother R. and Brother G. was out shopping together at the mall
Now, Brother R. was one of those more holy and righteous than you all
He took his purchase to the cash register to be checked
Watched the sales clerk and flicked
Every time the keys went peck peck
The bill came to 20.95.
He opened his wallet and took out the dollars
A total of twenty-five, handing it to the clerk
She gave him back twenty dollars.
He quickly stuck it in the pocket of his shirt.
He hurried out the door
Before she could she could discover the error, saying,
"What a blessing, for a minute my pocket book experienced real terror."
But Brother G. said, "You know that's not right."
But he insisted God had blessed him through her oversight.

Now, blessings are not to be had
At the wrong expense of others,
So if this happens to you,
Give it back my brother.

Honesty is the best policy. We should never increase at the expense of others' dishonesty. Speak the truth in our hearts. Do unto others, as we will have them to do unto us.

Don't Let It Be Said

Oh Children of the Lord, truly the day of the lord draws nigh.
Get yourselves ready to meet him when he parts the sky,
Don't let it be said, "Lord, you know I worked for you, I gave you all my time."
I know you worked but it was not for me
I saw your heart and motive and here is what I've seen:
You loved to be in the limelight, receiving praises of men,
But your spirit was as dry as a cracker, cold as ice cream;
Dead as frozen chicken, you've never accepted my Son.
So the way that you are talking, is leading you to death.
Your good works are all defiled by your filthy heart,
Only true repentance can save you, not what you think is right
A new life I'll give to you, which is clean in every part.
So humble yourself before me and I'll save you by my might.

Message—there is such a thing as too late, so live for God while you have your being, he is ready to live through you as your life, just yield yourself to him. He calleth just answer and say yes to him while it is yet today. Harden no our heart. His yoke is easy and his burdens are light.

Hos 10:12, Ps 89:47, Romans 13:11, 2 Cor 6:23, 1 Cor 6:2, Rev 10, Matthew 11:28

Children

A blessing from the Lord are they
Training them in the Lord to his glory
Is not always an easy way
Yes generation upon generation
There are children welfare and care,
Their parents struggle underneath the burden
Of meeting the needs they have to bear.
Children, be thankful to the Lord for parents,
Whose life you share
A mother and a father who give you such good care.
Children be obedient,
Your parents have your interest at hand,
Raising you right is their aim
Live out all your days
Enjoy the good of the land.

Children you will not always be.
You are getting older each day.
The young girl will be a woman,
The boy, a man becomes he,

So children enjoy your parents while you can,
Their heritage is your gain
Because someday the responsibility
Of taking care of you
Becomes yours to claim.

It is a blessing to have children, they are God's heritage: even if you were not the parent of your own, and you helped nurture children, consider yourself blessed.

Romans 8:16, Matthew 19:14, Ephesians 6:1

The Hurting People

A people of despair amidst the human race,
Who are they you ask?
The hurting people
The poor as well as the rich.
So many needs and problems they are facing
In some ways they all are sick.

See their faces,
See the agonizing look of despair,
Who will lend a helping hand?
Or take a share of the burden
And show that they care?

Why, there is a little child
Will no one show him love?
There is a drunk man out in the street
Seemly all so carefully avoids
How desperate he groans
How for him our creator's love
Desires to be shown.
Sickness comes in many forms
Affecting the spirit, soul and body
Christ said, for the healing of the whole nation
Was his blood shed.

Jesus is the answer,
The truth and the way,
Accept his all you hurting people,
Why not do it today?

There will always be hurting people, for Jesus said in the world you will have tribulation but be of good cheer for he has overcome the world. He is still in touch with the feeling of our infirmities.

1Timothy 2:2, 1 Peter 4:9, Matthew 8:17

Joy

I have joy inside of me,
It bubbles forth in streams
And gushes of love
Lit by the fire of life
From heaven above.

How it flows when I praise
I worship my Lord,
Even in sorrow
I can still know
I am not left to odds.

Joy of joys I cant contain
It causes me to overflow and proclaim
Hallelujah
Bless his holy name.

Joy is the fruit of the Holy Spirit, it is the presence of God himself; In him there is fullness of joy and no sadness

Psalms 30:5, 51:12, 126:5, John 16:22, James 1:2

Life

My life lithe in the life of another person
That life contains my all and all
So I look beyond myself
And see the one who shall never fall.

He has hide me in himself
How wonderful that is to know
Day by day that life inside of me grows though my eyes fail to see it as so.
Aspects of that life daily I claim as my own
Reaching beyond a horizon of doubt and reasoning
Toward a shore of perfection
Because by faith
I know my life was born out of his resurrection.

God indwells us so that in him we move, live and have our being. So trust him depend upon him and he have you at heart.

Genesis 2:17, Deut. 30:15, Ps 16:11 36:9, Proverbs 4:23

Oh Child Of Mine

Oh child of mine,
My love for you is so great
It cost the life of my Son.
He gave it up willingly,
A pleasing sacrifice,
An offering well done

Oh child of mine
Don't you rebel.
I care too much for your soul.
You are special to me
So choose life
Instead of an eternity of Hell
Oh child of mine
Walk with me day by day.
You can't go it alone
Don't become discouraged.
I am the life, the truth and the way.

Oh child of mine
I choose you to be my very own,
No devil in hell can pluck out out of my hand.
Just accept my love.
Everything I've done was for you.
Yes every seed I've ever sown.

How wonderful it is to be a child of God. His very own beloved child. We was purchased by him through the blood of Jesus. He loves us with an everlasting love.

Luke 9:48, 1 Kings 3:7, Psalm 131:2

Never Out Grow Love

Born into a world of need
Man gropes as his soul doth surely pleads
"Love Love me", says she
I've outgrown so many things
But never, never my need of thee."

Branded into the heard and every fiber of humanity
Though individually displayed or expressed
Man reaches toward love
Sometime through vanity
"I've outgrown," says he "so many things
But never, never my need of thee".

The search no matter how longing and diligently sought
The heart digs for life's buried treasure
Fulfilling its persistent thought
I'll outgrow so many things
But never, never my need of thee,
You are my very existence
Costly yet free.

We can not survive without love. Everyone craves for the reality of its care. The real source of love is from the father who loved us so much he sent his son to die that we might live.

John 3:16, 1 Cor. 13, John 14:21, John 15

First Impression

We all have our first impression
Of others that we meet.
Sometimes we make hasty judgments
As we watch them from head to feet.
It makes no difference where we are
Be it the church house or out on the street
Be careful when forming your opinions
Yes, be careful and discreet,
Stop passing judgment on everyone
You happen to greet.
Impression can fool you.
Opinions are not fool proof.
While you have your opinions
Remember the other fellow may feel the
Same towards you.
What you see through your mortal eyes
Can deceive you, yes certainly mislead you.
What you hear with your ears can be a lie.
Ask God to guide you,
Your little peanut brain
Is incapable alone
No matter how hard it tries.
On first impression be wise,
See them through holy eyes.
*Impression may influence us but we don't accept everything we see or feel
as reality. We should not lean to our own understanding or trust entirely
upon our judgments.*

Matthew 7:2, Luke 6:37, Ecc. 3:17, Is. 11:3

Rainy Day

If you are saving all your money for some rainy day,
You are sure to have many of them come your way.
Its all right to save some, by all means, put some away.
But don't put your trust in your money.
Just like quicksand it's deceptive in its sway.
Rain comes in different forms
Sometimes it's just a sprinkle, other times a storm.
It may have sunshine, it may have strong wind
One good blow, and it's your money's end.

Mr. Hard Time is no different, he's a robber too
He will call on you no matter how we think we are prepared
And know just what to do.
Sometimes he strips us, leaves us bare
So I am warning you, beware.

Rain may bring sickness and destroy our health
All the money we saved accumulative yes, our life, wealth
Comes up short, by far we see
Leaving us worse than we thought we would be.

Some rain is so strong, it will sweep you away
This poem is not discourage
Let God direct your money and live happily day by day.

It's not wrong to prepare for difficulties and hardship, but don't live in the frame of mind of expecting them. What you fear will come upon you. Depend upon the father. His wisdom and understanding will take you where your money won't.

Luke 6:38, Ec 1:1-16, Pro 6:6

Giving

If you find yourself being selfish and that dollar won't let you depart
Holding on to it so tight,
To get one out of you one would have to put up a fight.
Remember God said the earth is the Lord, the silver and the gold, so loose.
It is not yours to hold
If you find yourself at offering time,
Looking for only your change purse, holding back the dollar bills
Saying this is my money and I will give what I will.
Remember where the heart is you treasures will reveal,
Money will master you it will even cause you to steal,
Rob God or Kill?
If you find yourself lying in God's house
And saying I ain't got no money,
When you know you left your purse at home deliberate
Then it is not the end
Remember you going to give in account for the deeds we done.
We won't escape no not one
God expect us to give freely,
Its better to give than receive.
You can't carry it with you
You can't harvest if you don't sow
What you are hoarding up someone else may spend your share
Someone you don't even know, of someone you have no care

Give with simplicity the holy word says. Giving is necessary for a continued supply. We should have been taught to give from infancy. Life itself is based on giving in order to receive. Love gives and you will always enjoy abundance.

Pro 25:21, Ec 11:2

<u>Yesterday, Today, and Tomorrow</u>

Occasionally we reflect on yesterday
When the memories of it comes our way,
The good times, the failures,
But I refuse to remain in that state.
What happened yesterday is forever gone,
I must go on and I won't despair.

Today is mine to hold.
I must live it to the fullest using the faith God gave and be bold.
I can only enjoy it one moment at a time,
Soon it will be gone from me and no longer be mine.
Lord I pray that for you I let my little light shine.
Tomorrow will have a different story to tell, yet I have hope.
I don't know for sure I will see it but I must cope.
The fact that I don't know keeps me looking up to him.
When it's all over our earthly life is just a reflection of when
Or then a story of what has been.
We cant live in the past nor the future day.
We only have the present moment.
It holds but a glimpse and it too passes away.
Reflections are sometimes good, but not always so,
Enjoy the good ones and you continue to succeed and grow.

Note—Everyone reflects on their life story at sometime or another. We can never continue to go forward looking in the rearview mirror of life all the time. If you catch yourself reflecting let it be to thank God for all the many blessings he has bestowed upon you.

Ps 34:1, PS 62:8, Ps 106:3

Generational Heritage

There is a generational heritage passed down between the black race that's different from any others, taught down through the years by our fathers, mother, sisters and brothers.

It's a thing called bad luck. You even find it in the church. You will be surprised at some of things people believe. For the New Year, its good luck to cook some black eyes peas, don't let a lady to be the first to show up at your door on New Year's Day. That's bad luck they say. Let it be a man. It's the blessing way.

Watch that black cat. He may cross your trail. So many lies been told on that cat for being black enough to send a person to jail.

Don't split the tree, your mom may lose her breast. Let us walk on the same side of the tree that we may save her chest.

Don't bring them raw peanuts in my house, the only bad luck you may have, they may attract the mice.

Then there is a sign of this and a sign of that, from itchy left hand for the good news we about to receive, to the itchy right hand means some money we perceive. Bad luck shouldn't be in the Christian speech. Good luck either don't fit. God don't deal in luck, neither should we. Let's believe him, he is always with thee.

Some traditions should be forgotten. Bad luck omen is certainly one of them. We don't live by luck. But through Christ, all the families of the earth are blessed. Choose to wear the blessing rather than depending on luck. It is the better way

Ps 56:11, 61:4, 62:8,

Regrets

We all have regrets, they are part of life sphere,
Yes regret that cost us something during our sojourning here
Yesterday is gone and cannot be changed,
Learn from your mistakes, don't get bogged down in
If only I had not done it, much to my shame.
If only I hadn't spent all my money foolishly and did not save none
I could be rich now, yes I could have been the one.
If only I had been wise by now I would have owned my own house.
If I just had married Mary instead of Sue
I would have had some pretty children, maybe two.
If only I had waited until I was older to leave home
I could have made a better decision but I thought I was grown
And could not wait to get out on my own
Maybe I should not have moved so fast
Maybe I could have made my marriage last.
Why did I stay in NY State?
I wouldn't be living at such a fast rate.
Why did I have to insist on having my own way?
It nearly killed me and I regret it today
All the drinking and the partying made my life a living hell
But I wasn't trying to go there I just couldn't do so well,
But Jesus came in to my life and today I have a different story to tell
Forgetting those things that are behind me, make my regrets take on a different light.
All my regrets was a search for his life.
For I was empty inside to gain him I had to die to really come alive.

Regrets cause some not to live in the now. Don't let it happen to you. Forget those things behind you. Choose to live the good life. Choose Christ

Phil 3:13, James 1:24, Heb 13:16

That's Not The Way It Is

Some folks never agree on anything someone else say
No matter how clear the knowledge shine,
They only see it their way.
Though their way may be wrong,
They will argue with you hard
And ever so long.

Sometimes even if they are right
And you give your consent,
They'll switch sides,
Do a ninety-degree turn
Just so they can be different.
When will they learn?

Being different can be good but there is such a thing as being ridiculous.
When it only matter that you just have disagree to be disagreeable.

Pr 25:24, James 3:16, Acts 15:29, Phil 2:14, I Tim. 6:5

Johnny's Crime Lab

Johnny you been bad
Go to your room, you will be sad,
Johnny goes gloomy to his own crime lab
There is no homeboy to which he can share
But there is a game boy so what do he care.
There is a computer with a chair
Friends he can chat with are there,
No reason to pull out his hair
There is Ruby the lesbian and John who is gay
Some who talk about sex all day.
There is an eight ball he can question
So curious is he,
A head start in witchcraft he will be
He don't have to have an imaginary monster
There is a real one there,
He has but one eye, but he can see
Everywhere call T.V.
Under the mattress maybe
Something for boredom called drugs,
No need to suffer if he gets the urge.
There maybe even pornography of every class
Naked pictures hidden beneath the case of glass,
To satisfy the imagination
Suited to his situation.
There is that chemical set mom brought
Johnny practice making bombs, hear that loud noise,
Ask him how that blood got on his arms.

He heard you coming and managed to give you
A facial expression just filled with charm
You can go now Johnny, punishment is over
Did you really win?
Unless you remove his tools for his lab,
You only help prepared him for greater future sins.

Message—you are your child's best teacher. Train him up in the way he should go. With hold no the rod of correction from him. Chasten him

Pro 13:1, Pr 23:12, Pr 22:6, 1 Cor 13:11

My Tongue

Lord, by your Holy Spirit
Control this tongue of mine.
It must not be loosed,
And run wild,
Destroying everything in sight.
You created a creation so beautiful,
I'd love to see it remain so.
Lord, you word says in my tongue
Lieth both life and death,
So life I want to give,
Guide my words continually
The best seeds you have to offer
Those only let me sow.

Set a watch before my mouth and keep the doors of my lip is my prayer, dear Lord. I know the power of the tongue that knowledge is not enough Lord. Let your wisdom be ever present that I might always let my word be seasoned with grace.

Ps. 15:3, Ps 10:7, Ps. 12:3, 4, Ps. 34:13, Pr. 12:18, 19, Pr. 18:21

Enjoy The Moment

The time is the moment
Which means right now,
Learn to enjoy it.
Ask God to show you how.

For you can't live the future
You can't relive the past,
Few people take time
To enjoy the moment while it last.

Life is passing you by.
Worries and pressure of all kinds attack you
Because you have your mind
On things you don't know are going to happen
Before you are wondering what you are going to do,
Look at all the beauty around you
The great mysteries too.
Enjoy this moment it's here
Just for you!

Take time to enjoy life, rest in the Lord and the peace he gives will keep you. We only have the moment live it to the fullest, to keep stress away from the moment let greatness and confidence in the Lord be yours.

Proverbs 15:23, Isaiah 12:3, Ne 8:10

The Dollar

Oh, how we belittle the value of the dollar.
But let someone cheat us out of just one of them,
Se how loud we scream and holler.
It takes the dollar to live on
We earn it by our labor
The dollar represents you,
So you want what's yours
And so does your neighbor.

Though that dollar has the value
Of a certain amount of gold,
A stingy person will lose that dollar
No matter how strong to it he holds.

The dollar is only a small fraction
Of God's wealth.
Some lust so after it
They lose all their health.

Though the dollar has its place in our life,
Put God above that dollar bill
Let him control your every circumstance
For your every need he can fill.

Don't trust in your money or you will be defeated in life. The lovers of money be brought down. The value of money is determined by the one who controls it, God or Satan.

1 Timothy 6:10, 1 Thess. 2:5, Titus 1:7, Heb. 13:5

The Gossiper

A gossiper is a person
Who spends their time idling around
Living by the latest sights and sounds.
A word overheard
The gossiper quickly claims
Spreading rumors is the gossiper's constant game.

The gossiper lives from rumors to rumors
Repeating them is such a great feat,
Hearing a new one
Is like the good food you eat.

The garbage can of life
Is the gossiper's domain,
As long as there is the latest news to repeat,
The gossiper is satisfied there to remain

The telephone is the best tool
For a gossiper's labor.
The lines are always hot
Giving out information on all her neighbors.
Don't be a gossiper,
Some other profession you should choose,
While the gossipers have so much to give in life
They are the ones who lose.

Someone once said that an idle mind is the Devil's workshop, but to be a gossiper is to live at the lowest level of life. Actual it's a form of death because it destroys lives. He that keepeth his tongue will keep his soul from trouble.

Pro. 21:23, 13:2,3

Oodles of Noodles and Other Quick Foods

A cry from a hungry child may be different from our memory of yesteryear
but there is a quick solution don't you fear, oodles of noodles are here.
Some little child would starve to death if oodles of noodles wasn't on the
pantry shelf;
So don't knock them, those who don't care for them yourself.
All kinds of cereals with or without sugar or milk, makes up the little one's
diet.
So many kids have to fend for themselves, because of absentee parents you
trust them to fix it right.
Peanut butter and jelly sandwiches, cookies and ice cream
Will fill them up quick, loaded with sugar, a real personality changer
Lots of energy and maybe some head banging.
Candy in the candy dish out on the table in plain sight,
No limit on how many they eat, watch out they may soon lose all their
teeth.

Mom I am hungry, yes I know dear,
Put on your coats you kids, I will get the keys.
Let's go to MickeyDee's I am not cooking tonight.
I am tired another may say, let's order out.
Pizza and soda should do it with some extra topping.
I know I am spending extra money, but I haven't done the shopping.

Go and fix some microwave popcorn, do up a bag or two
We can all share them, put it in a bowl while we watch TV.
Put a few hotdogs in a pot, get a loaf of bread,
Add some ketchup and mustard, hand me the soda pop
Save the glasses, use the paper cups

Mom when are you going to cook, another might say
Boy you better get out of here and straighten up your look
There is some bologna and spice ham in the refrigerator and mayo on the
shelf

You better eat some of that or else.
Cheese and cracker is the runner up,
There is so many other noodles,
You can just add hot water to in its own cup.

Sweet Jiffy Mix has replaced old-fashioned corn bread,
Biscuits are not hand rolled anymore.
The art of making them is almost dead

Instant this and instant that, thank God for the microwave,
But if you haven't got one, don't panic
Stove top and oven pot pies got you saved

Sunday dinners maybe different too,
No home cooked meals,
No, no, no slaving over the stove
KFC to the rescue,
Served hot, even some biscuits and gravy for you.

If we keep going like we are going the art of home cooking may be lost
If we have become lazy the merchants will keep feeding us at a high cost.
It's cheaper most times to cook.
Buy the whole chicken and you might even get the feet,
Make soup and have enough to eat.

In this day that we live in instant meals are finding its way to our tables more and more. Some families don't know what it is to have a home cooked meal as well as family time together. I do thank God for the instant food especially Oodles of Noodles, for they are the staple of many children who wouldn't get anything else.

Ge 9:3, Eph 5:20, 1 Thess 5:18

I Am Fine Except

Sister L was a beautiful saint, one who loves God and was so full of life, with the light of the very Son in her eyes. On her way to church one day she met Sister S who was also on her way.
Sister L was the first to speak, said God bless you sister S. Haven't this been a lovely week? How are you today?

Sister S without hesitation replied I am fine except my head hurts, didn't sleep good last night, I am not seeing well my glasses broke, I cant get them fixed you know, I am out of work, my other money got cut off, my house mortgage is overdue, two of the kids is sick, I got a slip disc in my back, my arthritis is acting up. I got a phone call that scared me so bad I like to had a heart attack. Got a pain in my lower hip and cold sores on my lips. You know I stuck a nail in my foot had to go to the doctor, ain't had no money to pay the bill, my pressure is high still. My husband left me too. But I am trusting in the Lord, I know he will see me through, but that's not all let me tell you this . . . .

Sis L had all the complaining she could take, said hold it Sis S. There is one thing left for you to do. Make your funeral arrangement now for your family sake.

Message—Don't be a constant complainer. It is a habit you can well do without. People will come to avoid your company. Even your family will become tiresome of you at time. Let your words be a dripping honey that others may find comfort in your presence and season with much grace.

Pr. 15:23, Col 4:6, Matt 15:11, Eph 4:29-32

You Are A Star

God thought so much of stars
He gave them a name
He even used a star, his son
Jesus' birth to proclaim

You might not be a Hollywood star
Withal its glory and world renown fame
But you are a star who brings glory
To his precious name

You might not be a five star general
Sitting on a pedestal of shining glory
But God's grace is upon you and
Oh what a beauty he adds to your life story

You might not be a star up in the bright sky
But you guide others and attract them
There is no reason to be in wonder, why

You are a star in your own right
Shining so brilliant for others to see
Yes you are a star God's gift to others
For all eternity.

Message—You are a light in this dark world, so keep shining for God's glory. Others will be drawn to God through you.

Matt 5:13, 14, 1 Peter 2:9, 2:5, Col 1:22,23

What They Said . . . Wrong Choice

Reflecting back on my choice of a mate, Oh I remember the days and every date
And I remember every word my loved ones and friends said,
But their opinions didn't matter to my love filled head
He is not the one for you they said, but I was too blind to see,
I didn't care what they said, my mind was made up to the "t"
Who do they think they are? It's my life and I do what I want, can't they see?
They said do he have a job, or do you know his background?
I said girl he is handsome, muscular and strong,
Being with him makes me proud.
They said do he love you, or is it lust?
But my heart would beat so hard when I was with him
I thought it would bust.
Riding in his car, I felt like a queen, he had me captured all in my dreams
I said he is my man, I know, so my husband he will be
I know he will treat me right, and not be mean to me.
He loves me with all his heart, I believe it so I just can't let go
I sit there trying to convince myself
I saw what I wanted to see. I knew he wasn't all that,
But I made excuses for him so it could be.
Signs of selfishness I ignored
He is the choicest of the pick, the handsomest of them all
He holds the key to my heart, So what they said didn't matter after all.
No, no he was not all of that, so when we ended up married he beat me with a bat
Gave me two black eyes, laughed in my face and called me fat.
I had his babies and made him a home, he did me so wrong.
They say love is blind, well it has opened both my eyes and now I must go on.

He walked out the door one day, and didn't even look back
He has never written or called, yes I made the wrong choice
And though I am no longer blind, he is still on my mind
Its not that I can't get over him, I regret that I didn't listen
He wasn't worth the price I paid, because I wasn't listening to what they said.

Message—We make so many choices during our lifetime. Some choices are more important than others. In order to make the right ones we must have God's understanding and wisdom. It is available to us daily, we just have to ask. Some choices we made have been regrettable but we must not dwell on them. We have to trust God and move forward

Isa 7:15, Ps 7:16, Ps 25:12

Poverty Ain't Help Nobody

Poverty ain't help nobody my friend
You can't buy groceries
With a "God Bless You", and a great big grin.
You can't pay for medicine with a
"If you had just asked me Friday, I had it then"

Nobody can't get full off of what you ate,
Today or anytime as far as that goes
You can't say there is no corn,
And the shoes not hurting if they are not on your toes.

Poverty ain't help nobody though we
Try to justify the cause
If you cant enrich someone's life
Its better to say I am sorry,
Leave it alone that's all

Poverty ain't help nobody,
I tell you for goodness' sake
You say here is a peanut butter and jelly sandwich,
While you enjoy your T-bone steak.

You say just be thankful you got something at all
No complaint you should make
Poverty ain't help nobody, some of us is so greedy
We eat all the meat then chew up all the bones
Old Rover just sit there wagging his tail
Gets tired of being hungry and neglected,
And finally leaves home

Never show a hungry person
Where you store your food,
And not offer them a meal,

You get this mouth to watering
And you get mad if they steal.
Poverty ain't help nobody showing off all
The dresses you got on sale.

If you didn't buy them a outfit too,
Don't offer them your old clothes if
They wear a size five and you are
As big as a whale.
Nothing from nothing is still nothing,
No matter how you say it
Poverty ain't help nobody, I can't say it enough
So don't expect me to be satisfied with it
If you do that, just too tough.

Gods blessings are for me, his riches I expect
Take all the poverty you want
You can grow real big and be proud
Suffering you think for him and when
You get to heaven and see what you could have had,
You will be speechless, yet to see his face will make you glad.

Message—Money answereth all things you have to have it. There is a cost for all material things. God wants you to have all your needs met and even give you the desires of your Godly heart. But the love of money is the root of all evil.

Phil 4:19, Hebrew 4:16, I John 3:7

A Mother's Role

A mother plays a great part in shaping everyone's destiny,
For everyone that comes into the world has, or have had a mother
As you can surely see including you and me
From babyhood on through the childhood years and even the teen,
mothers teach, train and meet their needs.
Through many heartaches and tears she prays for them and helps calm
their fears.
She protects them with her very life. She is the referee that keeps them
out of strife.
A mother may fill many a pair of shoes
Or wear many a hats
What ever is needed she becomes that
A nurse, a doctor, a cook, a psychologist,
A repairman and a taxicab driver if she has it to do.
Sometimes it's real hard to let them leave the nest
But God gives her the grace knowing she has done her best.
Even though they maybe grown up by now,
They will always be her babies
Still, they may have strayed away far
But her heart keep them ever so near.
Mothers appreciate your God-given role
This is your day,
So celebrate yourself in your own special way
You have helped your children life unfold,
The troubles you seen, only God really knows.

We should all appreciate our mother's, God gave them to use to bring us up and discipline us according to his plan. Let us love and respect them for so great sacrifices and hardships they sometimes endured. Pray and be blessed it may just save your life.

Eph 6:1-4, Pr 7:1,2,4, Pr 13:13,14

People, People, People

People can sometimes be sort of weird, don't you agree?
Sometimes it's so hard to understand them and their views, you just can't
see.
Identifying with them sometimes you don't want to, their animal instinct,
Like nature makes it hard to do.
Some people have a sermon for you, the gospel according to self
It my way and not no one else and make a mountain out of every molehill
too.
And oh they know what you should do if it was me instead of you

The same thing they accuse you of, they are doing themselves
But they can only see the faults of someone else
Selfishness robs them of love, so no one can help them
Not even God above.
Knowledge may swell their head, others treat their loved ones
As if they was dead.
Your personal business, don't trust them with it.
They may be willing to spread, claiming they only done it
Because they was spirit-led. They said I told Sis Sue or Brother "R"
So they could pray for you to be able to stand.
Or they may claim nobody can do as they do
Or no one possessions as good as they one they have too
But wake up sisters and brothers and to your own self be true.

I am only dealing with the negative aspect,
So if this profile don't fit you, don't think you are a suspect.
But if you are guilty of the crime, I still have love for you in this heart of mine.
I will live and let live through the power His spirit gives.

People are different. We all know God in his wisdom created us with different personalities, for his way is variety. We are made in his image and likeness but we must allow that image to develop through the plan he have for our lives. Only then can we truly be the person he intends us to be.

Gen 1:26, 27, Gen 9:6, Romans 8:29, 1 Cor 11.7

Are You Some Folks?

Some folks can't rejoice when others get blessed
They fuss and fumble, rant and rave for in their mind, cannot find no rest
It should have been me they may even say,
Just wait till I have my day
Some folks never want to give another praise.
They cannot see how they deserve it and why.
But don't overlook them if you don't want to hear their voices raised
I am better than that, I don't want to boast or brag.
I don't want to toot my own horn,
But I am not chewing the rag

Some folks lives to be out front every time
No matter what the cause
If it please self they do it without a hesitation or even a pause
If it hadn't been for me, it wouldn't have got done
Yes it was my input the prize was won.

Some folks cannot even see your point
They only have eyes to see they things they want to see, no _____
It not that way you think you know
I know I have more experience than you, I am a lot smarter and older too.

Are you a some folks think things through and through
If we are selfish and refuse to put Christ first,
we find ourselves being a some folks
Many many times while sojourned on this earth.

*We don't have to fit the mold that everyone else fits but we can learn to live
and let live. Be considerate of others and let the love of Christ grace us.*

Phil 2:3, 1 Thess 5:13

You Can't Do It Yourself

You can't live by yourself
You are a empty vessel you see
You are a container that will be
Filled with a deity, either you
Will choose Jesus Christ as you Lord
Someone is going to occupy your life and fill that void.

Life is live from within,
Be it holiness or sin.
You are not the captain of your ship,
For proof of this is
Observe the words coming
From people's lips.

The choice is yours to make
Your days are numbered, make no mistake
God has provided a way for us to really live
The life of his son to us he gives.

*I can do all things through Christ, which strengthens me, for I choose to
live in him and have my being. I can do nothing of myself, not even breath.
I am dependent on Christ for only through him can I really live.*

Phil 4:19, 4:13, Ps 27

Because of His Life

I am fearfully and wonderfully made inside and out
Whether you understand me or agree
I know its true without a hesitation or a doubt

For you can see I have four eyes instead of just two
Not the glasses I wear on my face that I use to see right
But the eyes of my understanding that gives me a gift of second sight

I also have a wonderful sense of hearing,
But I appreciate so much more the inner ears where God speaks
And causes me to be wise and God-fearing.

My sense of touch has increased so very much,
It now reaches far and wide.
For I am touched with the feelings and compassion of my savior
For now I am his bride.

My taste is so sweet now for I am tasting how good God is
It continues to amaze me still.
The aroma of his smell is mine too,
A sweet smelling sacrifice paid for it all
Now my body is his body and I stand tall.

Message—We have a spiritual counterpart to the physical sense that comes from being Born Again. We are now a partaker of his divine nature.

Heb 5:14, Ps 34:8

Destined To Be Free

You are destined to be free
And soar as the butterfly
Your heavenly father put his own life in thee
As he is in this world, so are you
The scripture says you are extremely wealthy, truly blessed,
Highly favored and deeply loved in the beloved as provided by his grace

Some may flatter you or just plain old tell lies,
They may devalue you or make you cry
But your heavenly father has lifted you above their image of you
And you are not stopping and they wonder why
For in his eyes you have been put right and now you are his constant
delight.
He purchased your salvation
With his own precious blood,
His immeasurable love is being poured on you like a flood,
In his righteousness you have been clothed
Daily his benefits he does load
Trouble may come and trouble may go
Friends may turned out to be someone you only thought you knowed.
But God will be there for you, comfort you
No plight too difficult, he can't carry you through
Lift your head up high and view that Gospel light
And the events of life will shine ever so bright
For you are holy unblameable, irreproachable in Christ's own sight
So continue in the faith, believing him in the things he saith.
His gift of wisdom, sanctification and redemption on you as he has
bestowed

A path of righteousness he prepared you to only goeth
The difficulties of life will soon be over,
Just hold on trusting in his finish work to keep you strong,
May your days be great and you live long

Message—Jesus set us free by giving his life for us. He has given us everything that pertaineth to life.

The Test

When it seems you have done your best
And yet failed every one of life's circumstances and seemly every test
God is faithfully and patiently waiting
For your abandonment of the problem so he can give you his rest

Sometimes life just don't seem fair
Sometime it seems God isn't listening and just don't care,
But everything you go through he share.
Nothing is too difficult, nothing is too rare,
So remember he is always there

The tests in you life are just for a season
Our Lord allow them for a redeemed reason,
So don't give up, don't faint,
What seems impossible, it really ain't.

If we never have tests we wont know growth in measurements. We won't know endurances or strength. We are tested that we might know our character that develops through God's character within and others will know us as his representatives. Don't complain and grumble. Stand strong in the Lord and the power of his might.

Ec 3:18, 1Ch 29:17, Jer 9:7

You Are What You Think

"Thought materializes into things" is a Bible principle, as you know
They start little, but will grow and grow
Negative thoughts will produce negative results as it claim
Positive thoughts will produce results the same
So let's think right and glorify his name.

In order to think right you must be careful what you hear or see.
You can't spend all your time watching any old thing on TV
What you feed on you feed others, good or bad
Oh yes you will serve it, whether happy or sad.

What your heart produces is a direct result of what is there
Your motives are an important issue too
From what when and where you will do

*As a man thinketh in his heart so is he—a Biblical principle well proven.
We must have our mind transformed through God's word. Only through
the Holy Spirit can this be accomplished. Wrong thinking produces wrong
living. God is transforming me through his word daily.*

Pro 23:7, 1 Cor 13:5, Ph 3:4

Life Pitfalls

When it seems as if life throws you a curve ball
And you can't make a hit of it at all
There is a way out, God has redeemed us from
The effect of the sin of Adam's fall.
Trials may come and trials may go,
Your deliverance will only come
Through the truth you know
Buckle up and stand tall
You are more than a conqueror after all
What affect you might not affect me,
The vision I have may not be yours to see
My weakness might be your strength
I may can only go a mile
But you can travel a greater length
Don't judge me by my handling of life
Don't treat me by the standard you think I should have
As some other man's wife
I am a person in my own right
Judge me through God's sight
Life can really be great
If only on God we will wait,
If we learn to love all our days
We will never fail, no way
For love is from God himself
And he conquers all else.

Many are the afflictions of the righteous, the Lord will deliver us out of them all. Pitfalls may slow you down, but never stop. Strive through the strength of God. Because you are more than a conqueror.

Ps 59:16, Ps 50:15, Ps 41:1, Ps 27:5, Ps 91:15

Free To Be

You are free to be,
If in your heart you know you are different.
Don't imitate others or you will never be free.
God made you different that I can see,
So be yourself you are free to be.

If your expression of yourself is differently
What's that to me? We are two kinds of fruit
Drafted into the same tree.
Even though we are different
Together as we walk in love we can agree.

A hypocrite is someone who pretends to be what he is not
Why put on a good show outwardly while inside your soul's in rot.
You'll pay the price
Such a great one it is too,
So why not to yourself be true
And let your motives be pure in whatever you do.

We have a God given right to be an expression of himself. His creativity caused us to be different. He gave us a personality equipped as he saw fit. Celebrate who you are putting God first, who makes you free to be.

John 8:32, 33,36

The Testimony

It was Sunday Morning, what a beautiful testimony services was well on its way. They prayer had been said and the scripture read. "Praise the Lord and tell it," the Pastor said. Sister C. gave a testimony and said it was true. She thanked the Lord and she praised him too. Sister W. stood to her feet to tell of her blessing. She told of the things she had learned that week. "Tell it," the Pastor shouted again. Then Sister L. Said I've something to say. "Tell it," the Pastor cried looking like a real leader, she said my testimony is true but I have some horrible news for you. The pastor was sitting quite composed with his glasses resting on his nose. Said "Tell it Sister, tell it. I know how you feel. Go on and tell it you just keeping it real." Not knowing what she was going to say, he said, "Say it loud, say it proud. She said I don't know where to begin, but I've committed a horrible sin. "Go on and tell it," the Pastor said again. Ok, you said I can. I am here today but I am really beat. I haven't been able to sleep or eat. "Tell it Sister, you better tell and get your relief." Pastor T. came to call, I never realized that we would fall, but things got quickly out of hand. I didn't make a stand. Instead of stopping we buried our pride and up jumped Pastor T. real fast say "close it, close it, testimony service done to long lasted'.

Keep a good testimony and never bring shame upon the cause of Christ. Lead not others into shameful reproaches we are our brothers' and sister's keeper.

Read 2 Cor 1:12, Hebrews 11:5, 2 Timothy 1:8

Old Age

Oh yes, you sometimes laugh at me because you are young
But by and by you keep living, I'll make you hold your very tongue
You'll see it's not so funny when I am finally done.

Of me you seek to be free but cant you see
There is no way of getting away from me
For I am the very root of the tree,
Except you die young and shorten your days.
You can only know if you don't watch your ways

You may spend millions of dollars
But I am always around you neck
Like the dog and its collar
You try to prolong my time
But I'll come to you for my traveling
It won't cost you a dime

You may try to cover me over, hide me behind a make-up screen
But by and by my head you see, will always be seen

Then behind every pill you take, behind every pain you feel,
To others you may seem to be a fake
But you know that old age and its symptoms are fore real.

Yes young ones the wrinkles will appear,
Some women who was once real beauty queens they will tell you
There is no reason to boast or brag, for they was once beautiful
But now is old hags.

Some now dyes their hair but the gray always comes back to haunt them,
That hair that was once beautiful, black and glossy
Now looks like the foliage on the oak tree, short bald and mossy.
In some the mouth was once a perfect flashing gleaming white set of 32's,

That chewed their food through and through.
Then came the day when they had to make a choice of what to do,
Was is going to bare gums grinning back at you,
Or a top or bottom plate or a tooth or two?

Voices that was once eloquent and strong,
you talk about a conversational some could really carry on
But now their voice is broken and coarse,
Just barely above a whisper, but at least they have one you young chippers.
The eyes have failed with very little sight,
Often there is no knowledge of what is being looked at
Even with the glasses placed on the nose.
It seems there is little comfort or hope it will ever be right.
But now they are thankful for just that little sight.

Old age has its good advantages too. You have seen more, experienced and know more. Be thankful to get old. Thank God by the day, old ages is just a reminder you wasn't put here to stay.

Message—Spend your days wisely, live from an eternal aspect and God will be the length of your days and he will continue to renew your youth. We should learn how to number our days according to Psalm 90.

Just Because I Am Saved

Don't expect me to be perfect, that is never make a mistake, just because I am saved.

Don't try to condemn me because I express a little feeling of emotional rage.

Especially if you keep on provoking me when I am trying to keep the peace,

And stay away from sin's wage.

Don't expect me never at any time to defend myself, and just take everything you issued out.

Don't say I am not saved, because you dished out unkindness, but you cant take what came back out of my water spout.

Don't think I got the devil in me, because it takes two to tangle can't you see

And just because you keep using and abusing my love, then finally I say no more

Because God in heaven got it all on record above

Don't think I have lost all feeling because I am saved

And have received many healings

I hurt like you hurt, I value like you have values and much self worth

They are God-given so you see

Its his life that makes me

Don't expect me to smile or laugh all the time

For there may be a little rain in between the sunshine

So if for the moment I am hurting and experiencing a little pain

And there is a sigh and a groan,

Be patient with me as God carries me on you see I am not living by my goodness
I am living by Christ life,
So just because I am saved I got to have him as my grace and guide
And if I was good and perfect all the times I would probably be boastful and pride.

Salvation is a free gift given to us. We were not made to be doormats or punching bags for the devil. The righteous are to harmless as doves but wise as a serpent, bold as a lion. I put on the whole armor of God and I advance forward

Eph 2, Col 3